THE OFFICIAL RANGERS ANNUAL 2007

Written by Douglas Russell

A Grange Publication

Designed by Steven James.

ISBN No. 0-9550057-1-X

FOOTBALL
RANGERS
CLUB
READY
CARLING
JEREMY
CLEMENT

CONTENTS

FIRST TO SIXTEEN
A CHAMPIONS LEAGUE ADVENTURE

In early December last year, Rangers joined the elite of Europe when they booked a place in the last sixteen of the 2005/06 Champions League competition after finishing second in Group H, behind winners Inter Milan but ahead of both Artmedia Bratislava and Porto. The Ibrox club had become the very first Scottish team to reach the 'after Christmas' knock-out stages of Europe's premier club tournament.

This is the story of that historical achievement . . .

9 August 2005 – Champions League Qualifying Round
Anorthosis Famagusta 1 Rangers 2

Second half goals by Nacho Novo (from close range after keeper Giorgallides only managed to parry a spectacular Fernando Ricksen overhead strike) and Ricksen himself (a cool finish under the keeper following a delightful Prso reverse pass) were just enough to secure victory in the dusty GSP Stadium in Cyprus. Although the home side pulled one back almost immediately after the Dutchman's conversion, a superb Waterreus block from Kampantais right at the end meant a crucial away victory prior to the second leg at Ibrox.

Rangers: Waterreus, Pierre-Fanfan, Rodriguez, Andrews, Ball, Ricksen, Ferguson, Murray, Novo (Burke 80), Prso (Thompson 74) and Buffel (Lovenkrands 58)

24 August 2005 – Champions League Qualifying Round
Rangers 2 Anorthosis Famagusta 0

Surprisingly, it was the visitors who dominated proceedings early-on and player/manager Ketsbaia came close when he struck the post with a thunderous 30 yard drive. Rangers, however, opened the scoring after Novo supplied Thomas Buffel and the Belgian cutely lifted the ball over the advancing Giorgallides in goal to give his side an overall 3-1 advantage, settling the nerves of both players and fans alike. Early in the second period, Dado Prso supplied the icing on that qualifying round cake with a quite stunning right-foot shot from the edge of the box after bamboozling defender Katsavakis.

Rangers: Waterreus, Ricksen, Pierre-Fanfan, Rodriguez, Ball, Novo, Ferguson, Murray (Rae 85), Lovenkrands, Prso (Thompson 66) and Buffel (McCormack 73)

13 September 2005 – Champions League, Group H Game One
Rangers 3 FC Porto 2

In a match of truly epic proportions, Rangers led the champions of Portugal twice only to see Co Adriaanse's side draw level before Soto Kyrgiakos claimed the winner near the end and ensure a marvelous victory. McLeish's team had taken a 1-0 interval lead after Lovenkrands ignited Ibrox with a wonderful left foot shot following Ricksen's well-placed ball into the box. Then, after Pepe squared the game early in the second period, Prso lit the blue touch paper once again by bundling home from Hamed Namouchi's flick. That man Pepe claimed his second of the game (again from a corner) but the last deeds were blue in both colour and action when Kyrgiakos headed home from Ferguson's free kick to secure maximum points and leave Ibrox well and truly bouncing into the night.

Rangers: Waterreus, Ricksen, Rodriguez, Kyrgiakos, Bernard, Lovenkrands (Buffel 55), Ferguson, Murray, Namouchi (Novo 71), Jeffers (Thompson 83) and Prso

28 September 2005 – Champions League, Group H Game Two
Inter Milan 1 Rangers 0

The Scottish champions were unfortunate not to take a point from this San Siro clash with Roberto Mancini's giants of Inter Milan. Rangers played some excellent passing football throughout the ninety minutes in the near-deserted stadium (UEFA had 'closed' the ground following serious trouble last season during the clash with bitter rivals AC Milan) and created some decent chances. Ultimately, however, luck deserted them and they were beaten by Pizarro's free-kick early in the second period which took a cruel deflection off the defensive wall, spinning past Waterreus in goal.

Rangers: Waterreus, Ricksen, Kyrgiakos, Rodriguez, Bernard, Namouchi (Thompson 89), Ferguson, Murray (Nieto 83), Lovenkrands, Buffel (Jeffers 77) and Prso

19 October 2005 – Champions League, Group H Game Three
Rangers 0 Artmedia Bratislava 0

Considering the number of clear-cut, goal-scoring opportunities that Rangers created, this night should have ended with Artmedia (3-2 conquerors of Porto in Portugal remember) returning to Bratislava on the back of a comprehensive defeat. Keeper Cobej was certainly in the right place to deny Prso, Nieto, Namouchi, Kyrgiakos and Rodriguez in the first half but he really should have been beaten on at least two of those occasions. Although leading a somewhat charmed life, his second half save that prevented Bernard's 25 yard screamer from reaching the top corner was of the highest quality. Following this 0-0 stalemate, the halfway situation in Group H was: Inter Milan - 6 points, Rangers - 4 points, Artmedia - 4 points and Porto - 3 points.

Rangers: Waterreus, Ricksen, Rodriguez, Kyrgiakos (Andrews 58), Bernard, Namouchi (Burke 74), Hemdani, Ferguson, Lovenkrands, Nieto (Thompson 37) and Prso

1 November 2005 – Champions League, Group H Game Four
Artmedia Bratislava 2 Rangers 2

Despite taking the lead twice in the Petrzalka Stadium, the Ibrox men were held to a draw when shoddy defending proved costly. Rangers had gone ahead in just three minutes when Dado Prso's headed goal - following Hemdani's free-kick to the back post and Kyrgiakos' subsequent header across the area – delighted the travelling support. After Borbely's equaliser five minutes later, Stevie Thompson, from Prso's precise delivery, then headed Rangers in front just before the break. Artmedia's second was a real blow although Lovenkrands had a golden opportunity to write his name in the stars right at the end but he headed wide from six yards with the goal at his mercy.

Rangers: Waterreus, Hutton, Kyrgiakos, Rodriguez, Bernard (Murray 90), Ricksen, Hemdani, Ferguson, Lovenkrands, Thompson (Jeffers 69) and Prso

23 November 2005 – Champions League, Group H Game Five
FC Porto 1 Rangers 1

Alex McLeish's 4-1-4-1 defensive formation looked as if it might just pay dividends in Porto's Dragao Stadium – Waterreus was hardly tested in the first period - but Lopez's subsequent goal on the hour meant that all bets became redundant. Throwing caution to the wind, firstly Thompson and then both Ross McCormack and Chris Burke took to the field to enhance the attacking options and, with just seven minutes remaining, the strategy paid off when 19-year-old McCormack blasted home from Burke's headed knockdown. The home crowd were stunned into silence but not so the follow-followers whose Rangers anthems filled the night sky! A magnificent double stop by Waterreus right at the end meant that the Champions League dream was still alive with everything resting on the final group game with Inter Milan in Glasgow.

Rangers: Waterreus, Ricksen, Kyrgiakos, Andrews, Murray, Hemdani, Namouchi, Rae (Thompson 62), Ferguson, Lovenkrands (Burke 78) and Jeffers (McCormack 75)

6 December 2005 – Champions League, Group H Game Six
Rangers 1 Inter Milan 1

Although manager Mancini rested some key players (Figo and Veron amongst others), Inter Milan still fielded an impressive line-up of top talent and took the lead courtesy of Adriano when the Brazilian striker powered home a header from Mihajlovic's wicked corner after half an hour. Rangers' response was swift however and, minutes later, Thomas Buffel (thankfully back from injury) threaded a defence-splitting pass through to Peter Lovenkrands who finished decisively past Toldo in goal. Namouchi could have sealed victory near the end but he headed wide after Bob Malcolm's accurate delivery into the box. When news broke after the final whistle that Artmedia v Porto had ended goalless, Ibrox erupted in the knowledge that this 1-1 draw was enough to guarantee Rangers second place in the group and therefore take them into both the record books and the last sixteen of the 2005/06 competition.

Rangers: Waterreus, Ricksen, Kyrgiakos, Andrews, Murray, Burke, Malcolm, Ferguson, Namouchi, Buffel and Lovenkrands

22 February 2006 – Champions League Last Sixteen
Rangers 2 Villarreal 2

The impressive La Liga outfit Villarreal (winners of Group D ahead of Benfica, Lille and Manchester United) took an early lead from the penalty spot after Dado Prso had handled but battling Rangers equalised midway through the half courtesy of Peter Lovenkrands' stunning left-foot strike following a great run by Chris Burke. Diego Forlan then doubled the Spaniards' tally – in rather controversial offside/onside circumstances – shortly before the break. Finally, with less than ten minutes on the clock and the game seemingly lost to a superior team, Thomas Buffel had the stadium foundations shaking once again when defender Pena buried the Belgian's hopeful cross past an astonished Viera in goal. Rangers may have been outplayed on the night but their European dream was still alive.

Rangers: Waterreus, Hutton, Rodriguez, Kyrgiakos, Smith, Burke, Ferguson, Hemdani, Namouchi (Buffel 68), Prso (Boyd 88) and Lovenkrands (Novo 75)

7 March 2006 – Champions League Last Sixteen
Villarreal 1 Rangers 1

On a night of high drama in the El Madrigal stadium – which resembled a mini-Ibrox before, during and after the game - the Light Blues were just a whisker away from becoming the first Rangers team to win on Spanish soil since those legendary heroes back in 1972. Peter Lovenkrands (with his fourth Champions League goal of the campaign) netted in just 12 minutes to the delight of the huge travelling support but Arruabarrena cancelled-out this advantage with an equaliser early in the second half after the home side came more into the game. With no additional scoring, Villarreal thus progressed to the quarter-finals of the competition on the away goals ruling with Rangers left to ponder what might have been.

Rangers: Waterreus, Hutton, Kyrgiakos, Rodriguez, Murray, Burke (Novo 86), Hemdani, Ferguson, Namouchi, Buffel (Boyd 63) and Lovenkrands

The amazing journey had come to an end but Rangers and their loyal fans could look back on a hugely satisfying European adventure that, from the August 2005 start until the March 2006 finish, comprised a total of ten Champions League games of which only one was lost.

FROM BRITANNY
TO THE BLUES
Paul Le Guen's Career as Player and Manager

Playing Career

1983: Paul Le Guen joins First Division Brest.

1984: Professional debut as a midfielder.

1989: Signed by Nantes and fills the role of playmaker in the First Division side.

1991: Le Guen moves to Paris Saint-Germain.

1993: In addition to winning the French Cup with PSG, the player makes the first of 17 appearances for the national side.

1995: The double of League Cup and French Cup with PSG.

1996: Now filling the role of sweeper in the team, PSG knock Celtic out of the European Cup Winners' Cup (in the early stages of the tournament) prior to winning the trophy and, off the field, Le Guen passes his coaching exams at Clairefontaine.

1997: Another European Cup Winners' Cup final but on this occasion PSG lose 1-0 to Barcelona.

1998: The League Cup (for the second time) and the French Cup (for a third time) are his last trophies with PSG and Paul retires as a player – and club legend - after seven years and 478 appearances for the Parisian side. During his time in the French capital, PSG reach the semi-finals of European competitions in five consecutive seasons.

Managerial Career

1998: Begins coaching Stade Rennes where in due course he will develop players such as Shabani Nonda, Julien Escude and El Hadji Diouf into star names.

2000: Stade Rennes end the season fifth in Ligue 1 – the club's best position in 35 years of competition.

2001: Le Guen leaves Stade Rennes.

2002: Takes over from Jacques Santini at Olympique Lyon following the club's successful capture of the Ligue 1 title.

2003: Two-in-a-row for the club after he guides Lyon to the league championship.

2004: Now also successful in Europe's premier competition, the formidable Lyon reach the quarter-finals of the Champions League in the same season that the French title remains at Stade Gerland.

2005: Action replay with the Ligue 1 Championship (four-in-a-row) and quarter-final spot in the Champions League. Although Le Guen has become only the fourth coach in France to win three successive league titles, he decides not to extend his contract which expires at the end of June.

2006: Following a year out of the game, and after declining coaching offers from the likes of Lazio, Olympiakos, Auxerre, Monaco and Lokomotiv Moscow, Paul Le Guen becomes the 12th manager in the history of Glasgow Rangers Football Club and his three-year-deal is rightly celebrated by all fans of the club.

RANGERS FOOTBALL CLUB
READY
1873
RANGE
EXIT 10
EXIT 11
PlayStation 2
MasterCard
CHAMPI

S F.C.
1873
EXIT 13
EXIT 14
12
Heineken
Heineken
New FordFocus
Ford
Ford
LEAGUE
RANGERS FOOTBALL CLUB
READY

HEADLINE NEWS!

Rangers made the following headlines during Season 2005/06. What was the occasion? The clue is in the date!

1. **MOST WANTED MAN IN EUROPE CAUGHT AT LAST**
   Daily Mail, 13/3/06

2. **MERCURIAL MARVIN WORKS ANOTHER MIRACLE**
   Mail on Sunday, 30/4/06

3. **FIVE-GOAL RANGERS FLATTEN MINNOWS**
   Sunday Times, 8/1/06

4. **TEEN SPIRIT IS MAGIC POTION**
   Daily Mail, 24/11/05

5. **PRIDE JUST CAN'T NUMB ECK'S PAIN**
   Daily Mail, 8/3/06

6. **FLYAWAY PETER ON CLOUD NINE**
   Daily Mail, 12/12/05

7. **BOYD EXORCISES A EURO DEMON**
   Mail on Sunday, 12/3/06

8. **SO, WHO SAID I WAS A WINGER?**
   Mail on Sunday, 15/1/06

9. **IF YOU ARE A RANGERS PLAYER READING THIS, BE AFRAID, VERY AFRAID**
   Daily Mail, 17/4/06

10. **GREEK GIFT BREAKS WOEFUL PARS**
    Sunday Times, 26/3/06

Answers on page 62

BETWEEN 1 & 100

Every answer in this fun quiz is a number between one and a hundred. Easy? Maybe not!

1. Paul Le Guen was born in Pencran (Brittany) on March 1st, 19 - - ?

2. How many times have Rangers been crowned Scottish league champions?

3. The number of goals that Rangers have scored in the three finals of the European Cup Winners' Cup.

4. In the European Cup of 1963, the great Real Madrid proved far too strong for Rangers. How many goals did the Spanish giants score over the two legs?

5. How many times have Rangers won the domestic treble of League Cup, Scottish Cup and League Championship?

6. The year that Terry Butcher became the first Englishman to lift the League Cup was 19 - - ?

7. Rangers' record tally of goals in any game with Hibernian was back in Season 1898 / 99. How many did the Light Blues net that day?

8. Penalty king Johnny Hubbbard netted - - times from 68 spotkicks?

9. During his time as manager, Alex McLeish won silverware how many times?

10. The Ibrox main stand was opened on 1st January, 19 - - ?

Answers on page 62

THE RANGERS ANNUAL

PLAYER OF THE YEAR

THOMAS BUFFEL

So often the beating heart of the team - especially when filling his preferred role just off the main striker - Thomas Buffel enjoyed a fine 2005/06 campaign and takes the Rangers Annual Player of the Year accolade. Naturally one player does not make a team but it is worth noting that when the Belgian international missed several weeks of first-team action because of injury last season (the period from early October until early December) Rangers lost three, drew four and won only one of their eight domestic and European fixtures.

Buffel began 32 games last term, scoring 6 goals in the process. In the beginning, back in August, he netted crucial strikes in consecutive games when Celtic and Anorthosis Famagusta were the Ibrox opponents. The Old Firm goal (after ghosting between markers Petrov and Balde) was Rangers' second of the afternoon whereas the Champions League strike was the important opener on a night when, surprisingly, the visitors were in the ascendancy. Before falling victim to injury in October, Buffel's name was on the scoresheet an addditional three times with a brace in the 5-2 CIS Cup win over Clyde and another opener in the 5-1 Glasgow destruction of Dunfermline.

When he returned both to the fray and his best position in the side, the player was part of the Rangers team unbeaten throughout the winter months of December and January. For good measure during that time, Buffel netted the opener once again when, on this occasion, Dundee United were beaten in the SPL for the first time in two years.

Also certainly worth recalling are his contributions in the latter stages of Rangers' Champions League campaign with both Inter Milan and Villarreal. At Ibrox, against the Italians, his defence splitting pass created Lovenkrands' equaliser and, at the same venue after joining the game as a second half substitute in the clash with Villarreal, it was his cross that created the Juan Manuel Pena own goal. Two weeks later on Spanish soil in the El Madrigal stadium, it was Peter Lovenkrands who scored but only after keeper Sebastian Viera failed to hold Buffel's initial strike.

As the season neared its climax, the Belgian international claimed his last goal of the campaign - a goal that fell into the rather important category. At Tynecastle in mid-March, with both Rangers and Hearts still battling to secure the remaining Champions League spot, his second half leveller in the 1-1 draw kept his side in contention for that European place.

Thomas Buffel – The Rangers Annual Player of the Year for Season 2005/06.

THOMAS BUFFEL
RANGERS FOOTBALL CLUB
READY
CARLING

SEASON REVIEW 2005 - 2006

AUGUST

A positive start to any new league campaign is always welcome and Rangers duly delivered with a comfortable 3-0 win over Livingston. Goals from Prso, Pierre-Fanfan and Lovenkrands were more than enough on the day. Although the following week's display was not as impressive, Rangers' first-ever visit to the Caledonian Stadium to play Inverness CT ended with all three points tucked away thanks, mainly, to a fine goalkeeping display by Ronald Waterreus and Barry Ferguson's Prso-created goal, some twenty minutes before the end. Then, at Pittodrie, Rangers fought back exceptionally well after going 2-0 behind early-on and goals from Prso (a superb header from Fernando Ricksen's corner) and Lovenkrands (an extraordinary overhead bicycle kick) put them in the driving seat. However, the dismissal of Ricksen - following his second yellow card of the afternoon - turned the game Aberdeen's way and the home side claimed the winner three minutes from time with Smith's twenty-yard drive. For the record, Aberdeen's last league win over Rangers had been way back in April 1998.

The first Old Firm clash of the season was a controversial affair. With the game evenly balanced and neither side in the ascendancy, Alan Thompson was dismissed by referee Stuart Dougal for a dangerous tackle on Nacho Novo midway through the first period. Rangers then took control and Prso, despite the close attention of defender Telfer, opened the scoring with a glorious side-foot volley past Boruc following Marvin Andrews' pinpoint ball into the Celtic box. Belgian blue Thomas Buffel doubled the advantage early in the second half after squeezing between Balde and Petrov on his way to scoring. Later, after substitute Maloney had netted from the penalty spot, Novo returned the compliment (following Petrov's foul on Prso in the area) for a final score of 3-1.

Hibernian were the visitors for the last league outing in August but missed scoring opportunities came back to haunt McLeish's men when substitute Ivan Sproule netted for the Edinburgh side with 25 minutes left to play. The Ulsterman subsequently claimed another two, without reply, thus enabling his side to move ahead of Rangers in the SPL table.

SEPTEMBER

Away to Falkirk, Nacho Novo scored from the penalty spot after Buffel had his jersey pulled when ghosting into the opposition box. However, Bairns substitute McBreen equalised with a header late in the second period for a 1-1 share of the spoils. Rangers rallied the following week and dismissed Kilmarnock 3-0 at Ibrox with goals from Prso (a first half penalty), Ferguson (a low drive from close-in after good work by both Buffel and Lovenkrands) and an og by defender Greer as Prso was about to convert Ferguson's precise delivery across the face of the goal.

The following Tuesday night, Rangers began their defence of the CIS Cup with a 5-2 home win over Clyde although extra-time goals from Federico Nieto (2) and Marvin Andrews were required after a 2-2 score at the end of ninety minutes. Then, a third SPL game of the season was lost when unbeaten Hearts (the league-leaders) won 1-0 at Tynecastle to move eleven points ahead of the defending champions. Despite creating few real chances, the Ibrox side did have two strong penalty claims turned down by referee Kenny Clark.

OCTOBER

The fans were treated to a five goal/five star show when Dunfermline came calling at the beginning of October. First forty-five strikes from Buffel and Prso were enhanced when Nieto (after Hunt had pulled one back for the Pars), Lovenkrands and substitute Ross McCormack completed the 5-1 demolition of Jim Leishman's team. However, the inconsistent form returned at Tannadice with a 0-0 draw against Dundee United, unbeaten in their six most recent SPL clashes with Rangers.

Alex McLeish's 200th match in charge was the 2-0 victory over Motherwell. With barely a minute on the clock, Chris Burke scored his first Rangers goal since May 2004 before Lovenkrands, after the break, doubled the advantage following superb lead-up play by Prso, the talisman. Seemingly cruising to victory against bottom-of-the-league Livingston at Almondvale, Rangers surrendered a two-goal cushion when teenager Snodgrass claimed a second period double for a 2-2 share of the points. This result meant that Rangers had won only one of their six away league games this season. Three days later, there was little improvement and Inverness CT returned north after a 1-1 draw in Glasgow. Steven Thompson cancelled-out the visitors' lead with thirty-five minutes play still remaining but a winner could not be found.

NOVEMBER

Aberdeen spent most of the game defending in their own half but, nevertheless, Rangers failed to produce any real fireworks on Guy Fawkes Day and the match ended in a 0-0 Ibrox stalemate. The following Wednesday, a poor showing in the east end of Glasgow saw the team exit the CIS Cup after a 2-0 defeat at the hands of Celtic. Even worse was to follow at the same location when Rangers were humbled 3-0 in the league following another disappointing display. With grey skies rapidly turning black, a subsequent 2-1 defeat in the clash with Hibernian at Easter Road meant that McLeish's side (eight straight games without a victory) had recorded the worst sequence of results since the very formation of the club back in the 1870's.

DECEMBER

Two to the good against Falkirk at Ibrox (an Ireland og and Lovenkrands penalty), Rangers let the Stirlingshire outfit back into the game in the second half when John Hughes' side scored twice in the space of three minutes for a 2-2 final score. Next up was Kilmarnock at Rugby Park where Dane Lovenkrands (deployed as a lone striker) was on the score sheet yet again, becoming the first Ibrox player to record a hat-trick in over two years. His threesome comprised: a cool drive under Combe following Bob Malcolm's super pass, a thunderous drive from a tight angle and a close range finish after Buffel's marvelous, mesmerizing run. Rangers-bound Kris Boyd netted near the end to make it 3-2 on the day.

Peter Lovenkrands continued to impress and his fifth goal in three games was enough to defeat high-flying Hearts 1-0 at Ibrox the week before Christmas. Dominating from start to finish, this was one of the team's best performances of the season. A third successive SPL victory - for the first time since May 2005 - seemed to be on the cards at East End Park as Rangers led 3-2 well into stoppage time. However, a controversial penalty enabled Dunfermline to equalise seconds before the final whistle. Scorers that afternoon in Fife were Lovenkrands (a double that comprised a stunning strike from the edge of the box and a penalty kick conversion) and Chris Burke with a little piece of magic from the tightest of angles.

In their final game of a rollercoaster 2005, Rangers (with five Under 21s in the 18 man match squad) recorded a first SPL win over Dundee United in two years. Second period goals from Buffel (the beating heart of the side once again), substitute Thompson and man-of-the-moment Lovenkrands ensured a well-deserved happy Hogmanay for the Ibrox masses.

JANUARY

A Kris Boyd hat-trick in the 5-0 Scottish Cup tie with Peterhead warmed the fans on a cold Ibrox day before a hard-fought encounter at Fir Park was decided by Peter 'can't stop scoring' Lovenkrands and his volley from close range just after the interval. This precious 1-0 win over Motherwell was only the third time that Rangers had won away in the SPL since the start of the 2005/06 campaign. Considering the chances that Rangers created in the first forty-five minutes of their next league game, bottom of the league Livingston were most fortunate to be only one goal down at the break. Scorer Kris Boyd then hit a second - shortly after Vincze had equalised for the visitors - before a late double from returning-to-fitness substitute Dado Prso sealed a comfortable (in the end) 4-1 win.

January came to a close with a Sunday away day in the Highlands – and another double from Kris Boyd. Inverness CT (unbeaten in 11 games) once again provided stern opposition but Boyd's brace and a Marvin Andrews' header were just enough for a close-fought 3-2 win. Following this victory, Rangers (now unbeaten in 10 matches) moved above Hibernian to occupy third spot in the SPL table.

FEBRUARY

In the Scottish Cup, Hibernian kept Rangers at bay throughout the first half and then delivered three killer blows in the next period to achieve their second 3-0 Ibrox victory of the domestic campaign. Then, four days later at Pittodrie, further ground was lost in the league race following a 2-0 defeat by Aberdeen. There was little joy back in Glasgow the following Sunday when the fourth Old Firm clash of the season ended with a 1-0 Ibrox loss although the three young Rangers Scots – Alan Hutton, Steven Smith and Chris Burke – all acquitted themselves very well. Interestingly, this was the first time that Celtic had managed a clean sheet since their November SPL clash with Rangers.

Hibernian subsequently provided the opposition for the second time in two weeks but on this occasion McLeish's men (with both Julien Rodriguez and Brahim Hemdani restored to the starting line-up) carved out a convincing 2-0 win following goals from Boyd and Ferguson. Another plus point on the day was a quite wonderful man-of-the-match display by winger Burke.

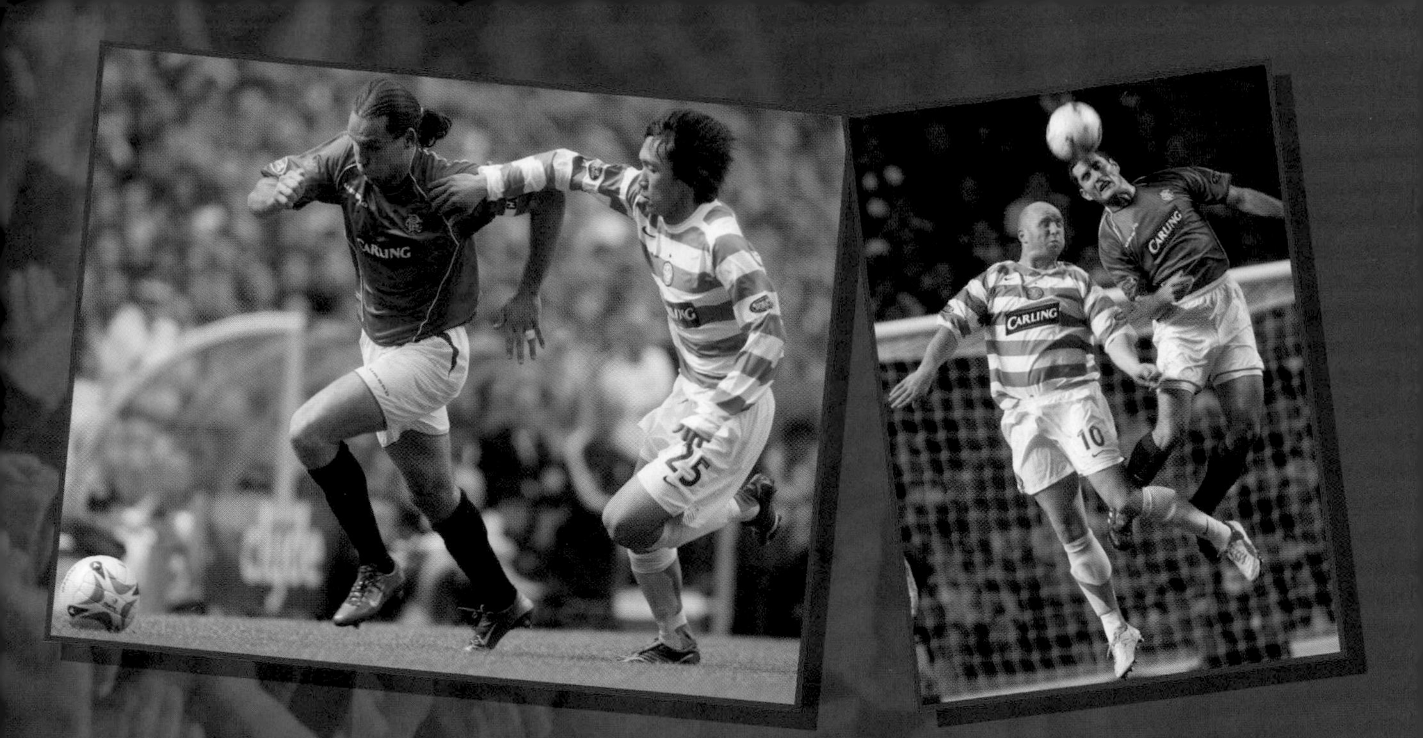

MARCH

It took a Twaddle own goal to seal all three points at the Falkirk Stadium after Kris Boyd's second half opener was cancelled-out by ex-Ranger Latapy's equaliser in a scrappy affair. The following week, Boyd's early strike – his 27th goal of the season – was the first of four against Kilmarnock at Ibrox. Subsequent goals from Rodriguez, Prso and Lovenkrands completed the emphatic 4-0 win. The gap between Hearts and Rangers remained six points following the 1-1 Gorgie Road draw as a second half Thomas Buffel conversion (from close range) nullified Jankauskas' early opener.

Dunfermline's 1-0 Ibrox defeat suggested a close game but in truth Rangers dominated from start to finish although it took a second half Kyrgiakos header to actually separate the sides.

APRIL

The last time a Rangers team won at Tannadice was in August 2003 but defeat was never an option on a Sunday afternoon when the Light Blues turned on the style for an impressive 4-1 victory. Dado Prso's fine all-round display included the opening goal (a terrific right-foot drive after twisting and turning on the edge of the box) but Kris Boyd was also a man-of-the-match candidate with the second hat-trick of his Rangers career.

Goalkeeper Ronald Waterreus produced two stunning stops before and after striker Boyd netted his 11th Rangers SPL goal in the 1-0 win over Motherwell, the last game prior to the league split. The following week, Boyd netted yet again but his second half, penalty box shot against Aberdeen was cancelled-out when Severin's drive was diverted past Waterreus by the unlucky Rodriguez for a 1-1 share of the spoils. Although Rangers had the better of the chances at Celtic Park during the next game, the final Old Firm clash of the season ended 0-0.

Then, at Rugby Park, a somewhat unlikely hero emerged from the shadows when Rangers were 1-0 down. Second half substitute Marvin Andrews not only equalised but also claimed a third after Kris Boyd had given his side the lead. All goals in the 3-1 victory over Kilmarnock were from headers and this was the first time that Rangers had come from behind to win in the SPL this season.

MAY

Easter Road has never been an easy venue but a Kris Boyd double sent the fans smiling into the night following a 2-1 win. His second of the evening (and 18th for the club) was claimed within a minute of Hibernian's equaliser - a Hemdani own goal from Riordan's free-kick. Dado Prso, incidentally, was the architect of both Rangers goals.

Although there was little but pride at stake for the final clash of the SPL campaign against Hearts at Ibrox, Kris Boyd ended the first chapter of his Ibrox career exactly the same way he started it – with goals! The striker's brace in the 2-0 win ensured his position as top scorer, having hit the back of the net 20 times since joining the club in January 2006.

SEASON STATISTICS
AT A GLANCE

Scottish Premier League

Played: 38
Won: 21
Drew: 10
Lost: 7
Points: 73
Goals For: 67
Goals Against: 37
Goal Difference: +30
Position: 3rd

Top Scorers

Kris Boyd: 20
Peter Lovenkrands: 18
Dado Prso: 12
Thomas Buffel: 6
Barry Ferguson: 5

First Team Appearances

Ronald Waterreus: 49
Barry Ferguson: 45
Sotirios Kyrgiakos: 39
Ian Murray: 37
Dado Prso: 36
Peter Lovenkrands: 35
Thomas Buffel: 32
Fernando Ricksen: 30
Chris Burke: 30
Julien Rodriguez: 29

RANGERS FOOTBALL CLUB
READY

Scottish Cup

After beating Peterhead 5-0 at home, Rangers went out to Hibernian following a 3-0 Ibrox reversal.

CIS League Cup

Defeated Clyde 5-2 at Ibrox before losing 2-0 away to Celtic.

Champions League

Reached the last sixteen after finishing second in Group H behind Inter Milan but ahead of both Artmedia Bratislava and Porto. Eventually lost on away goals to Villarreal of Spain after 2-2 (home) and 1-1 (away) draws.

Awards

Rangers Players' Player of the Year: Chris Burke
Fans' Player of the Year: Chris Burke
John Greig Achievement Award: Chris Burke
Goal of the Season: Peter Lovenkrands v Villarreal, 22.2.06

NEW SIGNINGS

NEW SIGNINGS

LIBOR SIONKO

Czech right midfielder Libor Sionko became the first major signing of the Paul Le Guen era when he put pen to paper on a three-year Ibrox deal in May 2006 after spending two seasons in the Austrian Bundesliga with champions Austria Vienna. Earlier in his football career he was with Sparta Prague and, during a four year period in the land of his birth, won three championship medals. Last season, the 29-year-old star was again in impressive form and, although playmaker as opposed to goalscorer, netted five times in 30 appearances for Austria Vienna as the club dominated domestically, securing the double of league and cup. Two of those goals, incidentally, came in the crucial 3-1 derby win over fellow contenders and great local rivals Rapid Vienna. Previously, in Season 2004/05, he claimed another five strikes during a successful Champions League run when Austria Vienna made it all the way through to the quarter-final stage of the tournament, only to be then beaten by Parma on the away goals ruling. A fine crosser of the ball, his European experience also includes reaching both the second group phase (in 2001/02) and the knockout phase (in 2003/04) with Sparta Prague.

NEW SIGNINGS

NEW SIGNINGS

LIONEL LETIZI

In year 2000, after four seasons with French Ligue 1 club Metz, Lionel Letizi became one of his country's most famous and expensive goalkeepers when he joined top outfit Paris St-Germain in a £4million transfer deal. During his subsequent six years in the capital, the solid, reliable and very safe Letizi not only played in the Champions League – 12 games in Season 2000/01 and 6 matches in Season 2004/05 – but was also a member of the PSG side that lifted the French Cup in both 2004 and 2006. The goalkeeper (who has worn the blue of France four times) made 33 and 27 club appearances in 2004/05 and 2005/06 respectively and, indeed, was virtually an ever-present in the side throughout those two seasons. Although originally under contract until the summer of 2007, Paris St-Germain rewarded the player with a free transfer (following his six years fine service) prior to penning a two-year Ibrox deal.

PROUD TO BE A BEAR

CARLING
CARLING
RANGERS
FC PORTO
3
2
87

SCOTLAND
BELGIUM
FRANCE
SPAIN
TUNISIA
PLG
CARLING
Paul Le Guen
Julien Rodriguez
Brahim Hemdani
Thomas Buffel
Stefan Klos
Fernando Ricksen
Chris Burke

WORLD OF RANGERS

HOMELANDS OF THE TEAM PLAYERS

Barry Ferguson

Kris Boyd

Hamed Namouchi

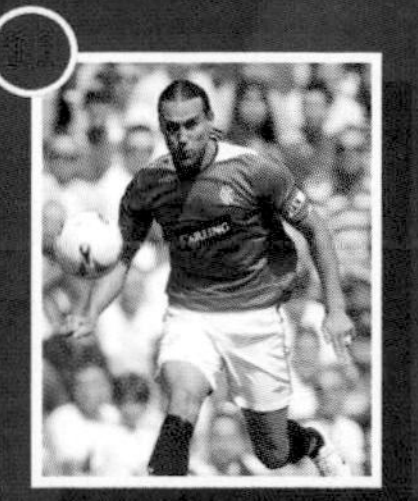
Dado Prso

Nacho Novo

Libor Sionko

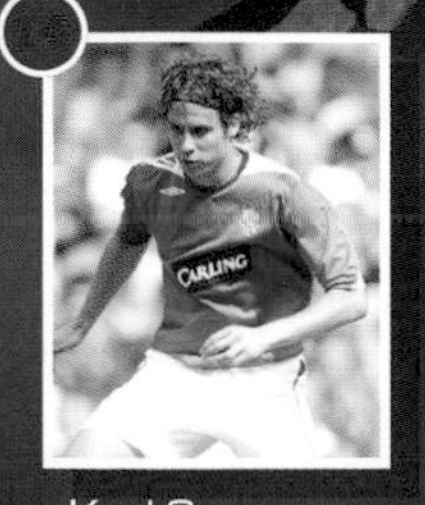
Karl Svensson

BARRY FERGUSON MBE

Never anything like fully fit during the latter stages of the league season because of a serious ankle problem, true blue Barry Ferguson constantly played through the pain barrier and bravely battled-on for several games before eventually having the necessary surgery towards the end of April. The midfielder, a player's player who always leads by example, started 45 domestic and European encounters games prior to an operation in Leeds by the same medical team used by the likes of Manchester United and Blackburn Rovers. Amazingly, after that ankle reconstructive surgery, it was confirmed that he had been playing for some time with snapped ligaments! Prior to hospitalisation, club captain Ferguson netted five times. His first strike - the winner and only goal of the game in the August away clash with Inverness CT - was followed by additional league goals against Kilmarnock at home (3-0, 17.9.05), Livingston away (2-2, 26.10.05), Hibernian away (1-2, 27.11.05) and Hibernian at home (2-0, 18.2.06). It goes without saying that an injury-free Barry Ferguson throughout period 2006/07 would be much more than just a mere bonus for Rangers.

STEFAN KLOS

The German goalkeeper received a hero's welcome from the Ibrox crowd when he made his first appearance of 2006, replacing the injured Ronald Waterreus for the late March home clash with Dunfermline. Rangers recorded a 1-0 win on the day (thanks to a second forty-five Kyrgiakos goal) but Der Goalie also played a major part in the close-fought victory with two stunning stops in the second half, before and after Rangers had taken the lead. Spreading himself, Klos' first save - from Mason - was of the highest quality but his injury-time stop when he leapt to push Tod's net-bound shot over the bar was even more impressive. In the last year of his current contract, he first arrived at Ibrox in December 1998 and, of course, has SPL championship medals from the periods when both Dick Advocaat and Alex McLeish managed the club. Klos missed the start of Season 2006/07 due to ligament damage to his right shoulder following a May bike accident in Switzerland.

ALAN HUTTON

Signed until year 2007, the young Scottish full back made his first appearance last term in the late October 1-1 home draw with Inverness CT when his contribution to the game included the cross that was converted by Steven Thompson for the equaliser and share of the SPL points. Hutton, back to full fitness after missing the latter part of 2004/05 and the initial segment of 2005/06 following his broken leg against Kilmarnock in February 2005, then filled the right defensive position for much of the remainder of that campaign before breaking a bone in his hand during the Rugby Park clash with Kilmarnock at the end of April. Earlier, on the Champions League stage, the youngster featured for Rangers in the three score-draw games with Artmedia of Bratislava and Villarreal of Spain.

STEVEN SMITH

A Murray Park graduate, Steven Smith is another young man who will surely benefit from his involvement in the club's wonderful Champions League run. Domestically, his first start was at Rugby Park pre-Christmas, replacing Hamed Namouchi in midfield for the 3-2 win over Kilmarnock. The following week, he played in his more natural full-back position when Rangers impressed again and defeated high-flying Hearts 1-0 at Ibrox. Interestingly, it was against the same Edinburgh opponents the previous season that Smith made his first-team debut when the 3-2 November win took Rangers to the top of the SPL tree for the first time in over a year. The Scot, who has the confident poise of a natural, more mature footballer, then featured in the first eleven an additional 16 times prior to the summer break and subsequent arrival of Paul Le Guen.

PLAYER PROFILES 2007

JULIEN RODRIGUEZ

Prior to signing for the club in August 2005, central defender Julien Rodriguez was a member of the Monaco side that reached the final of the Champions League competition in 2004. Indeed, the towering Frenchman was an ever-present for the whole of that campaign. His initial appearance for Rangers was actually in the same tournament when the Light Blues recorded a 2-1 qualifying round win in the away clash with Anorthosis Famagusta of Cyprus. Unfortunately, the fellow countryman of Paul Le Guen was hampered by injuries for part of his first year in Scotland but, from mid-February until the end of the season, he was virtually a constant fixture in the side, impressing the fans with his commanding defensive displays. It was during that period Rodriguez claimed his first ever Rangers goal – a strong penalty box header in the fine 4-0 March victory over Kilmarnock.

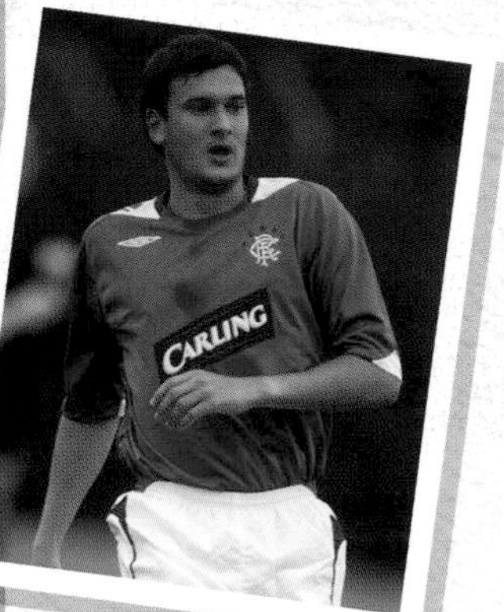

IAN MURRAY

The former Hibernian captain, now in his second year at Ibrox, was employed by manager Alex McLeish in a variety of defensive and midfield roles throughout the 2005/06 period and, from the very start of the campaign until the middle of October, was in the starting line-up for every domestic and European clash. Always hugely reliable and dependable (regardless of his position in the team), the versatile Murray is halfway through his initial three-year contract with Rangers and appeared in the starting line-up an impressive 37 times last season. Interestingly, only three players (Waterreus, Ferguson and Kyrgiakos) made more first team starts last term.

BRAHIM HEMDANI

The former captain of Marseille, Brahim Hemdani was another player whose first season was hampered by injury problems and it was late-on in the 2005/06 period before the Rangers fans had the opportunity to see him fully fit and at his obvious best. By the time that the SPL campaign ended in early May, the 28-year-old French-Algerian midfielder had started 23 games for the club. It is worth remembering that, prior to arriving in Scotland on a four-year-deal, Hemdani (a former French under-21 internationalist) had skippered Marseille all the way to the 2004 UEFA Cup Final.

CHARLIE ADAM

Charlie Adam enjoyed championship success last season when, on-loan to St Mirren, the central midfielder more than played his part when the Paisley side won the Division One title and, therefore, promotion to the SPL. This valuable experience will surely benefit the young player on his return to Ibrox. Possessing a super left foot, the youngster had actually made his Rangers first-team debut against Livingston in April 2004, followed by his first start the following month away to Dunfermline. Charlie's dad, by the way, wore the colours of both Dundee United and Partick Thistle during his own playing career.

CHRIS BURKE

There is no doubt that Chris Burke really came of age as a Rangers player last season when a whole series of wonderful wing displays both delighted and enthralled all fans of the club. Indeed, following one of his delightful, mazy runs at Ibrox in late February – albeit infield as opposed to out wide – Peter Lovenkrands struck to equalise against Villarreal in the Champions League. Talking of goals, the wee man (who could have joined Arsenal in his teens) actually scored himself three times in the 2005/06 period. His first two goals came in consecutive October SPL games with Motherwell (2-0) and Livingston (2-2) whereas the third was claimed at East End Park against Dunfermline on Boxing Day (3-3) when a superb strike from one of those 'impossible' angles stunned both follow-followers and Pars fans alike. His wonderful attitude to the game was perhaps best summed-up when, in late March 2006, he said in an interview: "I have always loved running with the ball and dribbling at people . . . I always want the ball. I just love playing football. That's why on the Saturday, I am always wanting it. When the final whistle goes, I am a bit gutted it's over."

GAVIN RAE

It is certainly an understatement to say that midfielder Gavin Rae has not enjoyed the best of times since arriving at the club after leaving Dundee in January 2004. However, one of the genuine delights of last season was the sight of the player - his long term injury problems thankfully now a thing of the past - once again wearing the blue of Rangers. After substitute appearances in the latter part of the campaign against the likes of Dundee United, Motherwell and Aberdeen, he subsequently made the starting eleven and turned in a man-of-the-match performance at Celtic Park in the final Old Firm clash of 2005/06. Rae, who with his previous club back in March 2001 had become the first Dens Park player to represent Scotland for some fifteen years, is the type of box-to-box footballer so crucial to any team in the modern game.

HAMED NAMOUCHI

A young man who has made marvellous progress since arriving in Glasgow from Cannes back in September 2003, he enjoyed an excellent 2005/06 Champions League campaign, with his powerful midfield presence a key element in Alex McLeish's European blueprint that ultimately saw Rangers make Scottish history by reaching the last sixteen of that prestigious tournament. Namouchi's total of seven starts in Europe was complemented by the exact same number of domestic appearances for the club. Impressive physically, Hamed Namouchi is under contract until 2008 and was in Germany as a member of the Tunisian national squad (the Carthage Eagles) for the 2006 World Cup competition.

NACHO NOVO

Top scorer remember with 25 goals in all 2004/05 competitions, the wee Spaniard had a frustrating time last season when injury seemed to be a constant partner at his side for much of that campaign. His 2005/06 year started well, however, with three goals in the first eight games. Novo's opener in the 2-1 Champions League clash in Cyprus against Anorthosis Famagusta was followed by two penalty conversions – Rangers' third in the 3-1 Old Firm Ibrox win and the opener at Falkirk when points were eventually dropped following a disappointing 1-1 draw. The striker ended the season having started only 13 domestic and European games for the club.

STRIKING WITH FORCE

KRIS BOYD

By the end of the 2005 / 06 campaign, Kris Boyd occupied a quite unique position in the history of Scottish football – he was top scorer with two different clubs in the same season! His 17 pre-Christmas goals for Kilmarnock, prior to signing a three-and-a-half-year Rangers deal at the turn of the year, were complemented by another 20 for the Ibrox club before the curtain fell in early May.

During his time at Rugby Park, Boyd had actually entered the club's record books when he scored all five goals in the 2004 5-2 win over Dundee United and, after transferring to Glasgow, he generously donated half of his Rangers signing-on fee to the Kilmarnock youth set-up. The strapping striker then became the first player since Colin Stein (in 1968) to claim a hat-trick on his Rangers debut when his threesome helped dispose of Peterhead 5-0 in the January Scottish Cup tie.

Two weeks later, a double in the 4-1 win over Livingston at home was followed by another brace in the 3-2 victory at the Caledonian Stadium when Inverness CT provided Sunday opposition in the Highlands. Further goals came at home to Hibernian (2-0, 18.2.06), away to Falkirk (2-1, 4.3.06) and at home to Kilmarnock (4-0, 11.3.06) before Boyd hit his first Rangers SPL hat- trick when Dundee United were comprehensively beaten 4-1 at Tannadice.

The powerful hitman, assured both in the air and on the deck, continued his scoring spree with goals against Aberdeen, Kilmarnock, Hibernian and Hearts after the traditional SPL split in mid-April. Indeed the clashes with the aforementioned Edinburgh clubs saw Boyd claim a double on each occasion thus ending his initial season in Govan with two hat-tricks and four twosomes to his name. At the end of the domestic campaign, Boyd was a member of the Scotland squad that jetted to Japan for the Kirin Cup tournament and, on his international debut in the opening game with Bulgaria, he scored twice in the 5-1 triumph.

It is worth noting that the striker (nominated in both the Players' Player of the Year and Young Player of the Year awards last term) only turned twenty-three in August 2006. Obviously still learning his craft, the best is surely yet to come despite those impressive goalscoring feats of last season. Now that is a thought!

KRIS BOYD

SPOT THE BALL!

SPOT THE DIFFERENCE!

Can you spot all ten?

Answers on page 62

WHAT'S IN A NAME?

Name the famous Rangers men who were also occasionally known as:

1. Captain Marvel & Captain Cutless

2. Tiger & The Rhino

3. The Wee Prime Minister, The Wee Barra & The Wee Blue Devil

4. Slim Jim & The Judge

5. Big Ben & Bomber

6. The Hammer & King Kai

7. The M & B Partnership

8. Blue Peter & The Moody Blue

9. The Goalie & The Doss

10. Jukebox, Jaws & Razor

Answers on page 62

THE EUROPEAN FINALS

Rangers have reached the final of the European Cup Winners' Cup on three separate occasions - at the end of Seasons 1960/61, 1966/67 and 1971/72. Following the club's superb run in the Champions League last winter, here's a reminder of those three earlier shots at glory on the European stage.

SEASON 1960/61

In May 1961, the Ibrox side became the first Scottish team to contest the final of any European competition when they faced Fiorentina to decide the destination of the inaugural European Cup Winners' Cup. Prior to the home and away two leg final, Rangers hit a rich vein of form (netting 19 goals on route) but the Italians proved just too strong at the last hurdle of both Glasgow and Florence games.

Rangers 4 Ferencvaros (Hungary) 2
(Millar 2, Davis, Brand)
Ferencvaros 2 Rangers 1
(Wilson)

Borussia M-Gladbach (W. Germany) 0 Rangers 3
(Millar, Scott, McMillan)
Rangers 8 Borussia M-Gladbach 0
(Brand 3, Millar 2, Baxter, Scott, Davis)

Rangers 2 Wolverhampton (England) 0
(Scott, Brand)
Wolverhampton 1 Rangers 1
(Scott)

Final : First Leg - Rangers 0 Fiorentina 2
Second Leg - Fiorentina 2 Rangers 1
(Scott)

SEASON 1966/67

After disposing of holders Borussia Dortmund in the second round, Rangers came so, so close to making it a Scottish-European double this season - Celtic had lifted the European Cup days earlier - but manager Scot Symon's men were narrowly beaten (after extra-time) despite having the best of the chances in the Nuremberg final against Germany's Bayern Munich.

Glentoran (N. Ireland) 1 Rangers 1
(McLean)
Rangers 4 Glentoran 0
(Johnston, D. Smith, Setterington, McLean)

Rangers 2 Borussia Dortmund (W. Germany) 1
(Johansen, A. Smith)
Borussia Dortmund 0 Rangers 0

Rangers 2 Real Zaragoza (Spain) 0
(D. Smith, Willoughby)
Real Zaragoza 2 Rangers 0
Rangers won on the toss of a coin

Slavia Sofia (Bulgaria) 0 Rangers 1
(Wilson)
Rangers 1 Slavia Sofia 0
(Henderson)

Final : Bayern Munich 1 Rangers 0

SEASON 1971/72

Five years later, revenge was the dish of the day as Rangers disposed of their 1967 conquerors Bayern Munich at the semi-final stage of the competition - 80,000 packed into Ibrox for the second leg - before heading south to the Nou Camp Stadium, Barcelona, Spain and a date with both Moscow Dynamo and destiny. Goals from Willie Johnston (a double) and Colin Stein on the night meant that, at last, a major European trophy would grace the Ibrox Trophy Room.

Rennes (France) 1 Rangers 1
(Johnston)
Rangers 1 Rennes 0
(McDonald)

Rangers 3 Sporting Club Lisbon (Portugal) 2
(Stein 2, Henderson)
Sporting Club Lisbon 4 Rangers 3
(Stein 2, Henderson)
Torino (Italy) 1 Rangers 1
(Johnston)
Rangers 1 Torino 0
(McDonald)

Bayern Munich (W. Germany) 1 Rangers 1
(Zobel og)
Rangers 2 Bayern Munich 0
(Jardine, Parlane)

Final: Moscow Dynamo 2 Rangers 3
(Johnston 2, Stein)

THE LETTERS OF RANGERS

Re-arrange the following letters and reveal the names of people, places and events associated with Rangers:

1. One of the truly great football managers :
LISA R WITH MULT

2. Field of dreams :
MI DAUXI BROTS

3. Will it ever happen again :
AIN IN WOREN

4. Paul is number twelve :
FRAME NOAGG NEARRS

5. The contents are priceless :
YOOR PORT HM

6. Season 2002/03 :
LE TESTED MC BIRO

7. Only the best have climbed it :
TASSEC AIR RAMBLE

8. The place to be in 1972 :
AN REAL COB

9. Green then blue :
NICE ROOMS TA HUNJ

10. Defence . . . and a half :
RUIC NON RITA

11. A home from home :
KEN MAH DRAPP

12. Perhaps at the end of Season 2006/07 :
HICS HISTONAC STOMP

13. First post war Rangers player to hit a ton :
INTO NORTH WELLI

14. Mini Ibrox, March 2006 :
MA LEAD GIRL

15. First to sixteen :
PEELIO GUNS MACHA

16. Talking about a revolution :
MEANS SEER SOUG

17. Thirty one and counting :
COPS SHUTS TIC

18. Number one player :
MAG ANY ROD

19. One half is certainly blue :
ROLF DIM

20. Goals was his middle name :
LIL SAMY TOCC

Answers on page 62

SUPER SEVEN

Any Rangers goal is cause for celebration so here are seven of the very best – and most important – from last season . . .

Dado Prso v Celtic, 20/8/05

The inspirational Ranger capped a man-of-the-match display in the first Old Firm meeting of the season with this exceptional strike. Following Barry Ferguson's pass to big Marvin Andrews, the defender launched a delightfully accurate ball into the box which Prso, drifting past Telfer, saw all the way. His subsequent right foot volley soared and whistled past Boruc in goal.

Thomas Buffel v Anorthosis Famagusta, 24/8/05

With the visitors somewhat surprisingly dominating the play and creating the best chances in this Champions League qualifier, Thomas Buffel's first half goal settled the nerves and eased the Ibrox tension on a night when so much was at stake. Keeper Georgallides could only watch as his advance towards the Belgian proved fruitless when Buffel, supplied by Novo, expertly lifted the ball over his head for the crucial opener.

Ross McCormack v Porto, 23/11/05

Youngster Ross McCormack ensured that his name would become part of Rangers folklore with this late equaliser. When fellow second half substitute Chris Burke headed a Ricksen delivery back across the opposition box, McCormack remained calm and focussed to fire home from six yards. That Champions League dream was still very much alive and kicking.

Peter Lovenkrands v Inter Milan, 6/12/05

The goal that took Rangers into the last sixteen of the 2005/06 Champions League competition – going where no other Scottish team had gone before. Although Buffel delivered a superb defence splitting pass, Lovenkrands still had it all to do as he raced through on goal but the Dane was poetry in motion and, with the other Italian defenders by this time mere spectators, he buried past Toldo between the sticks.

Peter Lovenkrands v Villarreal, 22/2/06

Quite simply, the goal of the season. With Villarreal on top and ahead through Riquelme's penalty conversion, Rangers were fighting for their Champions League lives when the ball broke to Lovenkrands following a lung-bursting Chris Burke run deep into Spanish territory. Barely taking breath, the Dane then, from some twenty yards, unleashed an unstoppable left foot drive that screamed beyond Viera.

Dado Prso v Dundee United, 2/4/05

For this first Rangers win at Tannadice since August 2003, the peerless Prso was once again quite immense and his goal, after leaving defender McCracken dizzily spinning and tied in knots, a deadly right foot shot high past Stillie.

Kris Boyd v Hibernian, 2/5/06

After putting his side ahead at Easter Road in the first forty-five, Rangers' top scorer for the season delivered another kris of life when he claimed the winner within a minute of Hibernian's second half equaliser. Fed by Prso, the striker retained his cool to despatch away from Malkowski for his second of the night and 18th in Rangers colours.

THE WARRIOR
DADO PRSO

Last season, Rangers had more than their fair share of injuries to crucial players but the loss of Croatian striker Dado Prso (from mid-November until mid-January) was a particularly cruel blow to the team. However, few would have anticipated the problems ahead when he scored the club's first SPL goal of the campaign against Livingston – a repeat of his feat the previous year when he also claimed the league opener in a game featuring the same opponents.

Prso then netted in three consecutive SPL and Champions League games against Aberdeen (2-3, 14.8.05), Celtic (3-1, 20.8.05) and Anorthosis Famagusta (24.8.05). His brave persistent play also ensured another Champions League goal in the astonishing 3-2 win over Porto of Portugal. For good measure, just four days later, he scored the opener - from the penalty spot - when visitors Kilmarnock were put to the sword 3-0 at Ibrox.

A further goal came in both the October 5-1 demolition of Dunfermline and, on European duty again, the 2-2 away draw to Artmedia Bratislava in the Petrzalka Stadium. Then, at Celtic Park in November, Prso was forced to withdraw during the game because of injury. The follow-followers would not be able to welcome back their talisman until he made a substitute appearance in the game with Livingston on 21st January. Though obviously not fully match fit, Prso nonetheless made a major contribution and late-on scored twice in the 4-1 triumph.

It was some weeks before the big man's next one - the game was the 4-0 home win over Kilmarnock in March – with his final goal of 2005/06 the opener at Tannadice against Dundee United (4-1, 2.4.06). However, for the remainder of the league campaign, Prso's inspirational play continued to enthral the fans and, for example, he was the architect of both Kris Boyd goals in Edinburgh for the penultimate SPL clash when Hibernian were beaten 2-1.

Speaking about the player prior to the last league game of the season against Hearts at Ibrox, departing manager Alex McLeish said : "I knew the minute I met him that he was a bit of a warrior. I knew he'd be in the trenches with us when we needed him. I think he quickly won over the Rangers fans from day one. I could see in his eyes and from the presence of the man that he was what we were lacking."

Every fan of the club would surely echo those sentiments.

DADO PRSO

LIBOR
SIONKO

FILIP SEBO

Slovakian striker Filip Sibo was a member of the Austria Vienna side last season that dominated domestically, achieving an Austrian Bundesliga and Cup double at the end of that 2005/06 period. The young footballer (he was born in February 1984) actually began his professional career with FC Koln in Germany before joining Inter Bratislava in 2003. His eight goals in twenty-five appearances for the Slovakian side won him a subsequent move to Artmedia Bratislava - one of Rangers' Group H opponents in the 2005/06 Champions League campaign - where he recorded a most impressive strike rate of 22 goals in 29 games. The hitman then joined Austria Vienna (for some £450,000) and subsequently hit the back of the net five times on the road to last season's double when he played alongside Libor Sionko. After winning a championship with Artmedia two seasons ago and one with Austria Vienna last season, Filip Sebo is obviously going for his own version of three-in-a-row in 2006/07 but this time, of course, he will be wearing the blue of Rangers.

A SEASON IN THE SUN

Season 1992/93 was a special time for all friends of Rangers. Number five of nine-in-a-row, the period comprised not only a domestic treble (for the fifth time in the club's history) but also a glorious, unbeaten run in the Champions League tournament. After losing away to Dundee in the fourth league match of the campaign (15/8/92), Walter Smith's men never tasted defeat in any competition until the following March – a quite remarkable run of 44 unbeaten fixtures that included 29 Scottish League games.

THE LEAGUE CUP

Having disposed of Dundee United 3-2 (winger Peter Huistra scored the extra-time winner at Tannadice) and St. Johnstone 3-1 (an Ally McCoist hat-trick) at the quarter-final and semi-final stage respectively, the destination of the season's first trophy was decided in late October when Rangers met Aberdeen at Hampden in the final of the League Cup. Goals from Stuart McCall and an og by defender Smith ensured a 2-1 victory on the day.

THE LEAGUE CHAMPIONSHIP

By the time that Rangers secured the Championship following a 1-0 early May win over Airdrie at Broomfield, the side had lost just two league games . . . and netted 94 goals! The irrepressible Ally McCoist (European Golden Boot winner for consecutive seasons) was top scorer with 34 goals despite having missed several games from April onwards after breaking his leg on duty with Scotland in Lisbon. Mark Hateley also made a major contribution with 21 goals of his own.

THE SCOTTISH CUP

Due to the reconstruction work at Hampden, both the semi-final and final of the Scottish Cup were played at Celtic Park. After Rangers defeated Hearts 2-1 at the penultimate stage of the competition, Aberdeen (runners-up in the league) remained the final hurdle between the Ibrox club and another triple crown. Goals from young midfielder Neil Murray and hitman Hateley were enough to secure a 2-1 win and treble glory for the fifth time.

THE CHAMPIONS LEAGUE

With both the Danish and English champions beaten home and away (Lyngby 2-0/1-0 and Leeds United 2-1/ 2-1), Rangers progressed to join Olympique Marseille, FC Bruges and CSKA Moscow in Group A of the Champions League. An unbeaten sequence of two wins (1-0 away to CSKA and 2-1 at home to Bruges) and four drawn ties was not quite enough to take Smith's side to the final but it was a famous undefeated journey nonetheless.

In football terms, the sun never really stopped shining all year.

McEWAN'S LAGER
Carlsberg
Admiral
TENNENTS
PREMIER ALLOYS
DIAL OFFICE SYSTEMS
ACORN
BONCOURT

NEW SIGNINGS

KARL SVENSSON

Prior to joining Sweden's World Cup squad in the summer of 2006, powerful 6ft 2in central defender Karl Svensson became Paul Le Guen's fifth signing, following the earlier recruitment of Czech Libor Sionko from Austria Vienna, French youngsters William Stranger and Antoine Ponroy from Rennes and South African youngster Dean Furman from Chelsea. The 22-year-old had spent two successful years with Gothenburg where his impressive play brought him not only the captaincy of the club but also his first international appearance for Sweden at the beginning of 2006. After agreeing a three-year contract, Svennson said ' I know that Jonas Thern and Jocky Bjorkland really enjoyed their time with Rangers and they did well when they were there. I haven't had a chance to speak to either of them but I don't need to. My mind was easily made up.'

NEW SIGNINGS

JEREMY CLEMENT

Highly rated by manager Paul Le Guen, the left-sided French midfielder celebrated his 22nd birthday a month early when he joined Rangers from Lyon in July 2006 following a £1 million plus transfer deal. At the time, Yves Colleu, Le Guen's assistant, said, 'I believe that Jeremy can bring more quality to the squad. He is a very good, young player with good technique and good skill. We need this kind of player here at Ibrox.' Although Clement only featured rarely for Gerard Houllier's Lyon side last term (a total of six starts with an additional nine substitute appearances), he was an integral part of the side during the previous campaign when Le Guen guided the Stade Gerland team to their fourth - and the manager's third - consecutive Ligue 1 Championship in Season 2004/05. Jeremy Clement's first team debut for Lyon had been back in early 2004.

OFFICIAL YOUNG SUPPORTERS CLUB

The OYSC is a fantastic supporters' club for Rangers fans aged 16 and under. Remember only official OYSC members have the opportunity to become matchday mascots and lead the team out onto the pitch. Members are also chosen at random to attend exclusive player events such as signing sessions and Q&A sessions.

Every member receives a membership pack that includes, amongst other goodies, OYSC bootbag, wrist wallet, bouncy ball, stickers, both birthday and Christmas cards at the appropriate time of the year, Football in the Community money off voucher and a fun-filled 24-page newsletter issued three times a year.

Other exclusive benefits include free entry to certain SPL home games (with a paying adult), free entry to the Rangers Tour Experience (with a paying adult), 5% discount on Rangers merchandise in all JJB Stores and, subject to availability, free entry to Under-21 games. Best of all, each and every member is automatically entered into amazing 'money can't buy' competitions like the following from last season:

OYSC VISIT TO HIGHBURY, HOME OF ARSENAL

20 lucky members were selected to attend the North London derby between Arsenal and Tottenham Hotspur in April 2006. Their prize included return flights to London, match ticket and exclusive behind the scenes tour, London Eye flight, Pizza Express meal and overnight hotel accommodation. The winners also met some of the Arsenal squad!

CHAMPIONS LEAGUE CENTRE CIRCLE STARBALL

30 members were chosen to wave the Starball before each of the four home games with Porto, Artmedia Bratislava, Inter Milan and Villarreal. The 120 lucky winners in total obviously had an unforgettable experience!

SIGNING SESSION

100 OYSC members of all ages met Chris Burke, Kris Boyd and Steven Smith when the players posed for pictures and signed autographs.

25 MASCOTS

OYSC members are selected at random to be matchday mascots with two chosen for each home game. However, when Rangers played Artmedia Bratislava at Ibrox in the Champions League, 25 OYSC members were chosen to be mascots – one for each player and official – and given a full Rangers kit!

Ready to join? Just call 0870 600 1972, visit www.rangers.co.uk or pop into any Ranger shop.

Back Row : Ian McGuiness, John Wright, Jose Pierre-Fanfan, Hamed Namouchi, Marvin Andrews, Dado Prso, Karl Svensson, Alan Hutton, Ian Murray, Kris Boyd, Davey Lavery, Davie Henderson.

Middle Row : Jimmy Bell, Olivier Bernard, Makhtar N'Diaye, William Stanger, Charlie Adam, Stefan Klos, Lionel Letizi, Allan McGregor, Julien Rodriguez, Antoine Ponroy, Brahim Hemdani, Bob Malcolm, Billy Thomson.

Front Row : Joel Le Hir, Chris Burke, Nacho Novo, Thomas Buffel, Barry Ferguson, Paul Le Guen, Yves Colleu, Gavin Rae, Jeremy Clement, Stevie Smith, Libor Sionko, Stephane Wiertelak.

QUIZ ANSWERS

PAGE 16 - HEADLINE NEWS!

1. Paul Le Guen confirmed as manager of Rangers. / 2. Second half substitute Marvin Andrews scores twice in the 3-1 away victory at Kilmarnock. / 3. The 5-0 Scottish Cup win over Peterhead. / 4. Substitute Ross McCormack and his crucial Champions League goal in Oporto. / 5. Rangers go so close to European glory in Spain against Villarreal. / 6. Peter Lovenkrands' hat-trick in the 3-2 Rugby Park win over Kilmarnock. / 7. Kris Boyd scores against Kilmarnock four days after missing a good chance in the Champions League clash with Villarreal. / 8. Peter Lovenkrands confirming that he never played wide before joining Rangers. / 9. Prior to arriving at Ibrox, a superbly fit Paul Le Guen completes the 'Marathon des Sables' – a fiercely gruelling seven-day, 250 kilometres desert run. / 10. Sotirios Kyrgiakos claims the only goal of the game against an ultra-defensive Dunfermline.

PAGE 17 - BETWEEN 1 & 100

1. 64 / 2. 51 / 3. 4 (1 in 1960 / 61 and 3 in 1971 / 72) / 4. 7 (1 in Glasgow and 6 in Madrid) / 5. 7 / 6. 86 / 7. 10 (10 - 0 final score) / 8. 65 / 9. 7 / 10. 29

PAGE 42 - SPOT THE BALL

PAGE 42 - SPOT THE DIFFERENCE

PAGE 43 - WHAT'S IN A NAME?

1. John Greig and Bobby Shearer / 2. Jock Shaw and Don Kitchenbrand / 3. Ian McMillan, Willie Henderson and Alan Morton / 4. Jim Baxter and Ally McCoist / 5. Willie Woodburn and John Brown / 6. Jorg Albertz and Kai Johansen / 7. Jimmy Millar and Ralph Brand / 8. Peter Huistra and Davie Cooper / 9. Andy Goram and Jerry Dawson / 10. Gordon Durie, Tom Forsyth and Ray Wilkins

PAGE 53 - THE LETTERS OF RANGERS

1. William Struth / 2. Ibrox Stadium / 3. Nine in a row / 4. Manager of Rangers / 5. Trophy Room / 6. Domestic Treble / 7. Marble Staircase / 8. Barcelona / 9. Maurice Johnston / 10. Iron Curtain / 11. Hampden Park / 12. Scottish Champions / 13. Willie Thornton / 14. El Madrigal / 15. Champions League / 16. Graeme Souness / 17. Scottish Cups / 18. Andy Goram / 19. Old Firm / 20. Ally McCoist